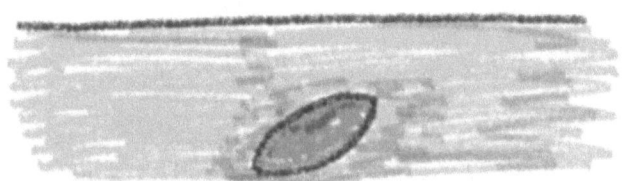

Why do I feel so much?

Like the waves are crashing in

Why do I feel everything?

I wish I could make it stop

But sometimes I feel nothing

I stare and feel numb

Everything or nothing... what's better?

Everything or nothing at all

A flood or desert

A feast, or a famine

Night or day

Lost or found

Am I numb or am I lying to myself?

One

One day, you will wake up and it won't be so hard to get out of bed.

One day, each hill won't feel like a mountain.

One day, you won't feel so alone.

IT GETS BETTER.

One breath at a time, until it doesn't feel so heavy,

one step at a time, until you don't feel so lost

YOU WILL BE FOUND.

One day, one more time.

One more puppy wiggle

One more best friend giggle

- You have more
- It gets better
- You will be found

Give it one.

One day

One breath

One step

One more

For every past, present, and future version of me and you. May you have courage to "give it one".

Dear You,

From my heart and thousands that came before me, I welcome you into my heart.

I've always said that poetry is the language of the heart. If we gave the heart a microphone, instead of the rhythmic beats, we would hear a flow of words that echo love, loss, and everything in between.

At 16 years old, everything was a question mark. I couldn't fathom deciding my entire life when I was grappling for the first time that it ends.

I've always felt alone in how much I was feeling or how sometimes I would feel everything, while other times nothing at all. So I wrote to try and make sense of the feelings of not feeling good enough, of feeling lost, or of falling in love.

This collection of poems is an exploration of growing up, losing and finding yourself, heartbreak and the choice to get back up again.

Because time and time again, we fall. In love, apart, in place. We fall purposely into leaps of faith. Sometimes our arms are flailing and others we are braced for impact. But I believe it is in the act of falling where life happens and seasons change.

My hope is that you can travel through these words and be reminded that you are not alone in your feelings or that these words may bring you back to the warmth of what it felt like to fall in love— whether that love was fleeting, eternal, or somewhere in between.

I write this for you. And maybe, you can find some of yourself in these
pages.

- Isabella

Poems

1. The Beginning: Feeling Everything

Stupid Little Love
Dear Mr. Sandman
The Art of Hugs
Light as a Feather
It's Love
No Space for Grace
Leaving
Write Them Anyways

Worst of Me
"I guess I am going to
have to suffer"
Lost or Wandering
Metamorphosis
Cycle
Nobody Ever Told Me
Suddenly

2. The Fall: Breaking & Losing

I love you, scratch that I used to
With you, Wherever you go
Linger
Kick
Please Don't; Darling
The Years of Us
Million Little Pieces
Invincible
Haiku 1
The Way I am Now

3. The Rise: Building & Hoping

1. The Becoming: Healing & Growing

The Beginning: Feeling Everything

Purple Journal
01/2021

I don't know what to write tonight. I feel outside of my head. I tried to write a poem, but I stumbled here instead. My friend is dead, and I am here. I feel so much it's messing with my head. I'm either angry or blubbering, I haven't found any in between. Actually, that's false. Right now, in between. The numb. The feeling of great pain looming over my head. I can't think of tomorrow, I barely made it through today. I'm trying, I promise. I just don't know how to do this. I'm going to go to bed. I think I'm finally tired. Well actually I've been tired all day but maybe I got some thought out so for a couple hours I can rest my head. My poems sucked tonight, maybe tomorrow I will be able to write. But today they suck so I wrote here instead.

From my notes.
09/2024

I'M IN LOVE!! AND IT FEELS SO GOOD!!

Purple Journal
12/2020

Bold: don't be shy, Izzy. Ask the deep questions. Talk to people. Let your guard down.

Stupid Little Love,

Stupid little love

Why do you keep hurting me?

Attached to my identity

Chained to my sanity

What is the cost?

Of you and me

My stupid little love.

What defines me?

One

Two

Three

Another injury

No one hears me.

Hurting

Limping

Leaning on a crutch

Barely moving

Falling down and letting down… will the pressure consume me or

My stupid little love

Completing me.

Inspiring me.

Saving me.

The quality of faith

And a glimmer of hope

For my stupid little love

And for the moments that are meant to be mine

I'm not out of time

It's not time to say goodbye

One, two, three seconds it takes me

To fall back in love,

with my stupid little love

Dear Mr. Sandman,

Wide awake or fast asleep

drift away to the great escape

tales of horror or so much life

Do I want to see the morning light?

Close your eyes and hope to float

Dear Mr. Sandman pick me first

Dancing with the stars

or ruling the Earth

Please Mr. Sandman pick me first

No more hurt and only love

Thank you, Mr. Sandman, for picking me first

The Art of Hugs,

Best friends forever

I wrap around, love coursing

True and true by you

Magnets, we collide

Your arms wrapped around my waist

When two become one

It is you I need

Holding me, broken in fear

Whispers– I've got you

Uncertainty creeps

Walls grow higher and higher

Rumors abounding

It's happening now

Space between awkward feelings

Leaving unsettled

Memories grab hold

Securely reminding me

You are all I need

When it is all done

I run to your open arms

Where I'm meant to be

Light as a feather,

Light as a feather

Just trying to keep it together

Hungry but not

Small pieces so I don't get caught

Covering up

Trying not to slump

I hate the mirror

Always looking bigger

Will I be faster

Does it really matter

Other girls

Watch them twirl

I can barely stand

I don't understand

Light as a feather

Just trying to keep it together

It doesn't work long

At first you feel strong

And you smile when you look thinner

And you're not as hungry at dinner

But your also tired

And this is not desired

So when you start to go downhill...

It really did work until

Light as a feather

Just trying to keep it together

It's Love,

Laced in the air we breath

Intertwined with the beating of our hearts

Felt in the way he smiles

Heard in the sound of her laugh

Woven pieces

Sometimes broken pieces

A part that went missing

And suddenly when everything becomes whole

Indefinable

Unquantifiable

A need

A want

A burning passion

An answer to your question

A solution to the problem

A million little moments

A hope it lasts forever

When all that matters is for a second

A second in time

I get to love you

And you get to love me

When everything becomes clear

And there is nothing to fear

A warm rush

A feeling of full

That's when you know it's love.

No Space for Grace,

The beating of my heart goes faster than I ever will

I count one, two, in, out

Reminding myself to take in each breath

I focus my eyes ahead

Today is the day.

It has to be.

Images and feelings are flying though my head

Attempting to cling on to what's left of myself and the countless of scenarios laid out for me

I want it so badly

The things I have given up

Shaving off pieces of my skin

Left all cut up and bloody

At last I feel that familiar tingle in my bones

Soon to become prisoners

Chained to my hopes

Reality brings shock to my system

My body is snapped into position

Suddenly the world is quiet

It's the lub dubs that fill the void

Sewn together with needles in previously made holes

Everything disappears

I have nothing to fear

This one step of feeling chosen

Casts the broken

I am yanked hard from my seven minutes of heaven

Falling hard from cloud eight

I've never spent enough time to reach number nine

It doesn't matter the ending

There's never any space for grace.

Leaving,

It's the way I could close my eyes driving home

Or the smell from my family kitchen

The familiar faces when I go to the store

Or that one coffee shop who knows my order

A collection of favorites

I can't go anywhere without knowing I've been there before

It's been boring

And I've often had nothing to do

But I think I've taken for granted the way I call here… home

It's not just the places

And certainly not only things

It's a million different feelings that have given me a place to belong

The road where I got asked to prom

Or the parking lot we talked in for just a little to long

The way I can take just three roads and end up at your door

This is what I'll miss the most

The people who made this town a home

But while there is misery in the idea of leaving the known

I can't help but think of the way this new place could become a home

That maybe that stranger could be a friend

Or that place down the block could be my very own

And then home could become a little bigger

And I think that's totally okay

Write them anyways,

Sometimes life isn't so poetic

Sometimes it feels like the words are slowly slipping off the paper,

like the chapter won't end... and pages are left unturned.

How do you find the words if they weren't supposed to exist?

It's supposed to be straight,

but this isn't straight.

Is it poetic?

Or a little chaotic?

Help me find the vocab, teach me how to translate.

Where are the words?

What is the meaning?

Why am I lost?

Where do I go from here?

When you write about it, it becomes real.

and real is messy, curvy, unclear.

But real is real.

Real is not fake.

and this is fake.

We have to turn the page, because the book goes on,

even when the chapter ends.

Now, that's a little bit poetic, and a little bit chaotic.

So even when you can't find the words, **write them anyways.**

Worst of Me,

If I love the worst of you

would you love the worst of me

The shadow of a perfect person

Putting on a pretty face

Messy

Uncoordinated

Am I hard to love?

Would you get tired of dealing with worst of me?

Loving you is easy

I love every part of you

Every insecurity, every flaw

it makes me love you more

Do I love too much?

Would you want to be loved by me?

The whole me,

Or just the parts that are acceptable?

This poem is a narrative poem about two fictional characters Theo and Ana based on the works of Vincent Van Gogh, see index for more information on the inspiration behind this poem!

"I guess I am going to have to suffer",

It was among the irises
and in her favorite shoes
that I fell in love.

It was a series of small
things brought together
that created something
great and oh so tragic.

I wasn't certain of
anything but with you,
me and the stars I was
able to dream.

To passers-by it may
have seemed like just a
wisp of smoke but to me
it was a blazing flame.

I knew it would be
dangerous but what
would life be if we had
no courage to attempt
anything?

So I attempted

And the dangers swiftly
disappeared when she
smiled.

Her hair was the color of
sunflowers, flowing and
long but she was like the
sun.

Full of light, full of
her. It was like the
moment I saw her, the
entire rotation of my
world shifted.

Suddenly I was in orbit
around her.

It was artistic, loving
her.

The day where we sat
sorting through my
collection of baseball
cards is the day I told her
I loved her.

"Of course you do Theo"
she replied "it is good to
love many things"

I didn't know it then but that would be the beginning of the end.

It was in the night, so much more richly colored than the day, that I lost her.

It was under one of those starry nights that she told me that "for the good of it all" we were done.

The world went cold, like the sun had been snatched from the sky.

There were no more daisies. No more poppies. Just cold, dark nothingness.

It was strange for me to not find you when I came home in the afternoon.

It was odd when you didn't call to hear about my day.

It was devastating when I saw your golden hair bounce down the path we used to take to the meadow in the mountains.

Oh how the thought of you hurt for so long.

But oh how beautiful it was to love you, most people find too little beautiful.

My best friend told me one day something I'll never forget,

"Love is the best and most noble thing in the human heart, especially when it has been tried and tested"

Oh how Ana tested me but for a little while she loved me too.

The more you love, the more you suffer.

I guess I'm going to have to suffer.

Lost or Wandering,

Clear

There was green grass while baby blue wildflowers danced in the wind

The sun warmed the earth

Over this clear cut path

Easy.

The air was warm

When you would breath it gave want for life

The steps were simple on this clear cut path

A soft hum brought you back to earth

It wasn't difficult to open your eyes

The overcast sky above covered the sun

The air was cooler here

The path was sand and vaguely marked with rocks as it led to the coast

There the waves crashed into the shoreline

And for a second you wondered how it would feel to be underneath

Pressure.

The strength of being pulled under

Not knowing which way was up or down

For a moment a thought comes

Why fight?

Can't pressure be good…

Like a hug

Firm and secure

When everything falls into place

That first breath above water

Breath like the first scream of an infant

Salt in your eyes and chattering teeth

The world looks different from here

The shore or the ocean

The path most taken or the one in the dark

Pressure or purpose

Lost or wandering

Metamorphosis,

And there it was

Small but there

Glances saying a million words

Inching legs

A want for something more

A wonder

Some questions

It continued

Slow and building

Fattening and infatuating

Fuzzy feelings

Little laughs

Closer and closer

They walked

Deeper and deeper, conversations growing

A silky web

Spun together

Protecting from the storm

Time

Patience

A changing creature

When all at once suddenly broken free

Fluttering hearts

Moments not months

A metamorphosis of sorts

Awoken

Alive

Colorful and bright

To be continued

To be transformed

To be . . .

Cycle,

My hopes go up just to come crashing down

Like a roller coaster you're scared to look down

I wish you could get it right because I really want you around

I'm not a puppet or a cat obsessed with a string

I don't find it fun when you pull suddenly away

I know the feeling, the feeling of doubt

You train yourself to never expect so you don't get let down

But deep down inside you know you'll always be around because once in a moon it somehow works out

And there it goes again the cycle of hope and losing out

Nobody Ever Told Me,

Nobody ever told me about the feeling of being alone

It's all about the

Parties

The people

And the thrill of the unknown

But what do you do your house doesn't feel like a home

Somewhere new

with nowhere to cry

I feel like all I do is try

The piles of papers

It's never done

A decision for something greater

I promise I'm having fun!

It's the living free

And the people I've found here

But also wishing I could go back in time

To a town where I didn't feel like a stranger

And the welcoming smell of my childhood home

Confused with life

And no clear answers

Where am I supposed to go next?

Do we all feel this way?

So when somebody asks me I promise I will say

All the things nobody ever told me.

Suddenly,

In a matter of moments
life can change

In a matter of moments
everything goes dark

The lights won't turn on

They must be out

Who do you call when
it's just you in the dark?

The ringer won't ring

The breath has slowed

Suddenly life won't be
the same

Are we afraid of being
alone in the dark

Or not being alone, trying
to find our way?

Should we have to be
alone?

Suddenly a light appears.

A warm embrace

Suddenly life changed

But in a different way

Tomorrow isn't
guaranteed

But right now, is here

Life changes suddenly

But don't be afraid

Sometimes lights go out

And sometimes they turn
back on

Hold on a minute longer

Grasp that flashlight
tight

Because life changes
suddenly

So don't forget to search
for the light and hold on
tight

The Fall: Breaking and Building

Can't sleep notes
02/2023

I want my heart broken because then that means someone has had my heart for a little while and I've tried but why doesn't anyone want my heart? Am I secretly afraid for someone to have my heart?

From my notes
05/2022

Is it short-lived? How do I give without taking too much from me?

From my notes
12/2024

Where will I be in a year?

From my notes
09/2024

Sometimes I miss Isabella.

Can't sleep notes
08/2022

I want to be loved. Does anyone get butterflies when they see me? Anyone with crushes? I want someone to love each and every part of me.

I love you, scratch that,

I love you

Scratch that.

I used to love you

Or maybe I still do

I miss the way you used to make me feel

A burning passion inside

Always craving more

Did I crave too much?

Did I do something wrong?

Was I asking too much, when you decided to take it all away?

Try, try, and try again

If at first you don't succeed try, try, again

I think it goes something like that

That's not how it worked though

But I guess we never listened to the rules anyway

Breaking and Burning

Building and Healing

How many times can we be broken until we are unrecognizable?

I try not to care

But there's that word again

Try

Try again, hope again

Hope that this time will be different

That one of these days it will all amount to something

Because even when I don't care,

 I do

And even when I don't try,

 I do

So every time I come around to losing you,

I go ahead and love you.

"With You, Wherever You Go",

In loving memory of David Alexander (11/17/2003 - 10/27/2021)

And suddenly there was music and even more suddenly there was him

Charming, charismatic, carefree

The way he waltzed, the way he talked

It was magnetic

The tapping of human emotion

The level of energy

He loved people so easily

He danced and made it his mission for others too

Abruptly there was a fall

Maybe a misstep when the dance was changed

It was harder for him to find the rhythm

More difficult to pick up his feet

But you wouldn't know

Because he was still so beautiful

The way he lived

The way he looked

The way they were his safe place

The way he made us smile

The music was running out and the dance got slower

So he simply sat down and picked up his guitar

Fingers connected as if he was with us

Making the most of the time he had left

Right before the last note

He wondered what it would be like to love

But with a quiet whisper we said

You did

Linger,

Please stay awhile and linger at the door, I just need a little bit more

Don't tie your laces up just yet and please don't grab your coat

Stay a little bit longer and linger at my door

Sit down awhile, there's always room

Please sit down at my table scratched by toy lands that boarded up their doors

Come look at the stars before you go out to your car

Past the swings that flew us there, our feet now firmly planted on the ground

There's a whole big world out there
but once it was here in our heads and
in the stories we told

Please don't forget the lights always
on even when yours drives away

Stay awhile and linger at the door

I'll forever be waiting at this table
with a space saved for you

Kick,

In loving memory of Kassi Culp (06/26/2004 - 09/23/2020)

Sometimes I kick myself for living too much

When you're not living at all

I kick myself for love of life

When all you wanted was to leave

I kick myself for the warm embraces

When the world gave you cold

I kick myself for the excitement of waking up

When you prayed for nights

Every breathtakingly beautiful moment I realize you're not around to join the crowd

Every accomplishment

Wondering if you are proud

Birthdays a party of life are now just another reminder that you are not around

I'm wrong though

Every time someone gets wonder in their eyes, you smile

Knowing they're resting without the pain you knew so well

Hoping they get to reach the stars you didn't reach

And the plans you had to cancel

Every sunset, every sunrise

Every win, every loss

Every hope of tomorrow brings you relief that those you left behind are going to turn out just fine

You hope they understand the weight of the darkness and learn to carry a lantern

You hope they say I love you, knowing the hurt when it's too late

You hope they learned to ask the hard questions

You hope they have the courage to answer

You hope friends get together

And the ones who feel alone see that everyone has some type of battle they are fighting

You hope they learn that it's easier to fight with an army

You hope they don't go to bed mad and keep those who make their heart go pitter patter

You hope they are brave in the moments when it's easy to be weak

You hope they stay.

You know that one day hearts will be reunited and stories of the peaks and valleys will be shared

But you know that time can wait

But life can't

You're okay, you weren't but now you are.

And you know that the moments here are so few

So love and lose

Dream and make plans

Like the moments last forever

Don't forget to tell them

And don't forget to ask

Don't forget to do the things that make you feel something

Because it's better to feel than feel nothing at all

Feel and let go

Take the bad and the good and if it gets too bad

Let people who care take some, they care, someone cares

So I think instead of kicking myself for the life I get and you don't

I'll thank myself

I'll thank you

I'll thank them

I'll thank the sun when it rises

I'll thank the world for turning

I'll thank my legs for racing

I'll thank my brain for thinking

I'll thank my heart for loving

I'll make plans

I'll dream

I'll run

I'll write

I'll love

Even if it hurts, I'll live.

If you or someone you know is struggling with suicidal thoughts or ideations call or text **988** now or go to

https://**988**lifeline.org/ for **24/7** help and support

Please don't go; Darling,

Please don't go

Darling I am among the stars

Please don't go

Darling I'm the whistling of the wind

Please don't go

Darling I'm the fields of roses

Please don't go

Darling I'm the air you breath

Please don't go

Darling I'm with you every time you smile

Please don't go

Darling I'm right here

Please I can't let go

Darling you'll never be alone

Please I can't let go

Darling my love didn't leave

Please I can't let go

Darling you are life

Please I can't move on

Darling it's okay to grow

Please I can't move on

Darling you won't forget

Please stop the hurt

Darling, I love you

Please

♡

The Years of Us,

FALL:

We met in the fall, bright eyed and bold

Each one of us different, each with a different dream

But somewhere, somehow our paths finally decided to meet

Quickly and swiftly, we found each other

Merging like a river into the ocean

Solidifying as one

One unit, one team

Under the lights or on the court

We were together

There for every score

The first and last.

WINTER:

A daring flight, down the slopes we flew

Rosy cheeks

Big smiles

Warmed by fire light

We caught fire within us too

But when laughter filled the thin air

The tension was loosened, breaking the ice

Time would heal and even 17-year-olds grow.

Faced with decisions, my easiest was you.

SPRING:

As we turned our tassels, warm air blew in with echoes of last times and goodbyes.

This spring was different. Have a great summer, they said. Was it our last?

SUMMER:

Moods rising like the sun, but never setting

Days by the creek and nights under the stars

Fishing when we could and always in a bathing suit

Our greatest days, the build up

This was our free fall

FALL (once again):

The autumn came quicker that year

Goodbyes greeted by the crunch of the leaves

No knowing how to say goodbye, let go, or how tightly to
hold on…

But what remained, rooted deep,
was appreciation

for the time we had,
the acceptance of,
and our very best friends.

We held each other so tightly that day as if we were the
textbooks we used to press our saved flowers from prom.

Preserving the seasons of our youth, smooshed into the lines,
eyes blurry with our tears and the replaying of memories.

In some ways we still live in those pages, in the petals and
the crinkling fragments of our past.

But that was enough to make us forever.

Million Little Pieces,

I was whole once, but
then I broke into a
million little pieces

Shattered like glass
struck

When really I was the
one struck into a million
little pieces

A dark day

Extended into a dark
week

Into pitch black months

Alone in a world of noise

Putting on a smile to face
it

Wishing someone could
see the million little
pieces I was leaving
behind

Giving my pieces away

So others wouldn't have
to feel the blast

I was running out

I was tired

I didn't have much left

I was fine

I was healthy until I
wasn't

I was a good friend until I
wasn't

I was whole until I broke
into a million little pieces

Sitting in the pile of
brokenness I saw my
broken face

My broken heart

My broken mind

My broken smile

I saw something in those
million little pieces

I was worth putting back
together

That maybe

Just maybe

It was slow…. painful

But I slowly started to glue back the broken pieces

I lost some of myself in those million little pieces

I found some of myself in those million little pieces

When I stepped back I saw something that I couldn't before

We are all a million little pieces

Broken only to heal

Shattered only to be made whole

Picking up pieces of our lives we couldn't

possibly imagine living without

Standing in a shattered world

We are all made up of pieces

These are mine.

Invincible,

What do you say when a 17-year-old dies?

They lived a long life? They got to grow up? They did everything they dreamt to do?

What do you say when they haven't lived long enough?

How do you mourn when life is meant to go past high school?

There were no wrinkles around the eyes, no children to leave behind

Only a bunch of teenagers who have barely lived themselves

What do you say when he was supposed to be invincible?

This is what I would say

Hug them, tell them, kiss them

Give everything to the game

Don't stress about grades and eat more cake

Drive more with the windows down and dance in the streets

Forget and forgive

Dress how you want and roll out of bed

Party till dawn and always follow your dreams

Attract don't chase

Don't wait

Try that thing, show up

Care

He did, he cared. He lived. He did exactly what he was meant to do.

Live and remember why you do.

Remember what you get to do

Because he didn't get to

So

Mourn.

Cry.

Breakdown.

But live

Just like he did

That way he can really be invincible

It comes in waves dear

she told me on the shore

it is hurting now

The way I am Now,

The way I am now is not how I used to be

I think I am even different than I was yesterday

Different from the people who loved me and hurt me

Different from the choices I made

Different from every year I've lived

The way I am now pulls at me like a rope attached to my hip

While the person I was yesterday desperately clinging

Leaving scratches and indents of broken hearts and fleeting feelings

Swept away in a swift wave as I'm pulled along heels digging into old ways

Afraid of change

Why does it have to be this way?

The way I am now pulling me into fiery new ways flamed feelings and growing pains

My life flashes before my eyes attempting to remember the way I used to be and the molding of the way I am now

I wanted to be president

My mother packing my lunches

My brother's cheeky grin

The sound of my sisters laughs

And the way my dad used to hold me

Ex best friends

Old passions

The way they made me feel

Everything flashing and burning into bright embers, grey smoke circling me until one day

A breeze…

And I am the way I am now

The Rise: Building and Hoping

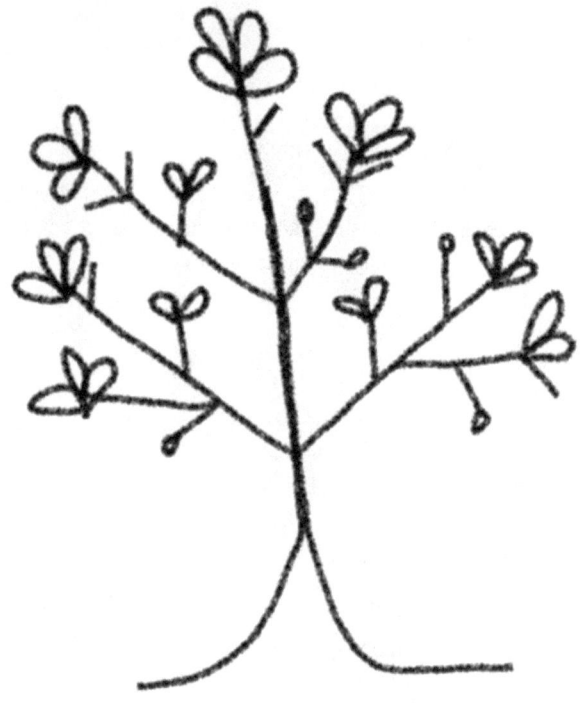

From my notes
02/2023

I have so much more love to give and so many more words to write. I have things I want to see and feelings I want to feel. There's so much food to eat and so much more laughing and crying.

From my notes
04/2023

After months of feeling like a shadow of myself. I finally feel like myself again. I can feel the light seeping in and everything becoming clearer.

From my notes
02/2025

When you give love it grows.

Pieces by iz love letter
06/2024

I think sometimes suddenly over little moments of hope, days you are just here, time, and growth things change. And there is a crack of light where there wasn't before.

Nothing ever remains the same,

To the tune of pouring rain

We moved our tassels

Throwing our caps in the air

Shouting we made it

Rushed into hugs

Colliding like our younger selves once did

In bustled hallways trying to make it to class

Have a great summer I said

But maybe I should of been saying having a great life

We were so blind to the fact it could ever remain the same.

This moment

when everything changed

And their lips touched

Silently saying everything they were afraid to say before

Small sparks suddenly into an ignited flame

not easily tamed

It was undeniable now

Everything had changed

In that moment

When everyone was wearing black and you weren't there

And I don't think I was either

Broken when you took a piece of my heart with you

Aching for your voice

Wondering how it could
ever be the same

This moment and every
moment beyond now

Different because I met
you

Shaken hands into a
shaken path

Where I know how you
take your coffee and you
know exactly what makes
me laugh

In this moment or any
moment

When you make a
decision knowing it will
never be the same but
choosing it anyways

The mourning of
yesterday and the hope
for tomorrow

Erased pictures you saw
for yourself

Suddenly into blank
pages

Because of one moment

When words are said and
chances are taken

When you looked at
me and when they
walked away

Everything changed

Because nothing ever remains the same.

Earthshine,

There is a side of me that
no one else knows

Tied to the darkness

Masked in the light of
day

Cratered and pitted

Impacted from the people
who came and stepped
afoot

Planting their flags

Leaving with evidence
that they had been there
before

But mostly this satellite
of mine remained a
desolate place

Only seen by those who
stuck around when the
sun disappeared beneath

It was special talent of
mine on how invisible I
could be

with feelings so unknown
to me

Cold, suffocating

Hungry and alone

Everyday the feeling
would grow as it slivered
into sight

as I danced in the day and
drowned in the night

For the first time, I felt
dull

while that side of me
shined until it was full

Full of the impacts of my
life

The footprints of my past

And the evidence of
myself

Realizing my moon was
every bit apart of me as
my earth

The earth of orange sunsets

And crashing oceans

Loud and creative

And worthy of love

It was a rhythm that kept me alive

Pulling into the shore and pushing out towards the waves

Locked in a perfect rotation

Until one day

ever. so. slowly.

the feeling.

started.

To shrink.

On another day when it was nearly gone and had just settled into a thin curve

It became one of the craters that made me

The phases of my moon

The rotations of my earth

Sprinkled with stars and moved by the breeze of summers day

This was me

In every phase

This was my earthshine.

The breeze takes the fuzz

I am wishing for you

a soft wispy love

Love Loudly,

We leave so many words unspoken

When feelings arise and no one moves a muscle

Scared of what some letters will do to the future

Settling for sleepless nights and constant wondering

You know what I say to that?

Love loudly.

Love like there isn't a timeline

Love without turning down the volume

Blare that stereo and sing the lyrics like the night isn't going to end

Buy her flowers

Tell him he looks handsome

Listen to your friend

Grab their hand and don't let go of the hugs that make you feel safe

Love like the buildings might crash in

Love with no limits

And don't only love them

Love you too

Love the way your hair falls

Or how you would never let anyone walk alone

Love the way you feel

Love even when no one is watching

And while your at it, love life too

Love how the sun sets in your favorite color

Or how you get to be right where you are

Love like the world depends on it

Because it does

So love loudly because you never know when you can't

So go

Tell them they are your favorite person and the stars look brighter when they are around

Don't turn down the volume

Love Loudly.

Dance,

I had been planning my whole life

Each move perfect and planned

A dance you could call it,

confident in each twirl

Every childhood dream

and each expectation met

But what was supposed to happen didn't.

There was silence

And an earth-shattering crash

a shrilling scream

And suddenly I couldn't see anything

Everything I had imagined before

Every planned move... Gone.

Sprawled out on this empty dance floor

Blinded in quiet

Each moment of before replaying in my head

Rewinding

Searching for what changed.

An idea. A dream. Me?

The person who I used to be and the person I wanted to be
could no longer exist together

But the me now, needed to get up

So in what felt like an eternity and a body-shaped indent on
the stone-cold floor

I lifted my body up into the silence

Each limb straightening then bending

Until I could walk and choose a new song

Soft music began to play

And instantaneously I started moving

with no planned moves at all

Now I wouldn't call it dancing,

and maybe I'll never be able to dance

But what was supposed to didn't, so now as I start over

I hope that what is supposed to, will.

The Sun,

We were supposed to rise
when the sun did

But we often did it so
much less beautiful

The sun always wanted
such a grand entrance

Every day

Spanning colors across
the sky

Could you believe it?

Every day it rose with the
expectation of
spectacular

Meanwhile sometimes I
couldn't even get out of
bed

Sometimes I didn't even
know if I would make it
to the sun's next show

But in almost spite of me

After an entire day of
beaming its golden rays

The sun spanned its
colors across the sky
AGAIN

As if once wasn't
enough

To remind me the day
was done

And then it was dark

Pitch black

Except for the stars

And while I could get lost
under their twinkling
lights

I often missed the sun

I dreamt of the oranges
and the reds

and especially the pinks

I wondered how the sun
would rise after we took
our slow rotation

This is what helped me
on my darkest nights

When the rotations were
the longest

Until one day when the
sun rose

I saw the day as a
beginning instead of a
slow end

There was now
possibility where there
was once none

And when the sun set that
night

I realized that it was not
in spite that the sun
colored the sky twice

It was a gentle reminder
that the day was over and
no matter how cold it felt

it could end warm

This helped me
appreciate the stars and
the friendly moon

It was in the silence, the
darkness

And in the colors

That I realized I wanted
to be around for every
grand entrance and be
there to appreciate each
end

Wish,

I don't wish you a storm but a day of warmth

I don't wish you poison but of sweetness softly spoken

I don't wish you fear but of serenity always near

I don't wish you sorrow but hope of tomorrow

When the stars are gone from the sky and the candlelight has died

I hope I'm heard by the moon

As I wish for you

Out of Nowhere,

The human is a hopeful being

Drunk on the possibly that today is the day that our wildest dreams come true

That love will heal our broken hearts and peace will restore the world

That the complicated will become simple and the hard, easy.

And sometimes it works

But most of the time it all comes crashing down

Piercing your skin

Piece by piece

Lying in shame, crying in pain

So why?

Why do we still continue to dream

To hope

When we know that sometimes we fall?

Because out of nowhere we fall in love

A normal day turns into your best day

Suddenly you feel okay

That feeling when it all falls into place

When you reach the peak and it is easier to breath

Something inside us changes

I don't know what it is but it makes forever seem not enough

So we remember that hug

the sparkle in their eyes

The painting in the sky

The butterflies

Those three little words

We keep photographs

We heal

We trust

We plan

AND we love

So that maybe today is the day that when I fall, I am caught.

The Becoming: Healing and Growing

From my notes
04/2023

It really did get better!!

From my notes
08/2024

There are some things you wonder if they really matter or if they count for something but a drive with the windows down with the wind soft against your skin and the sound of your favorite lyrics is something I've never wondered about.

From a stranger
07/2023

You make the world so much more beautiful.

From my notes
12/2024

They feel like coming home at the end of a long day.

Purple Journal
05/2022

I made it back to the other side. I made it back to me.

Love is...,

Is love perfect?

We are imperfect.

I know this

You know this

We are the essence of imperfection

So I think love has to be too.

And that's scary

Being imperfect.

Not being good enough

Looking in the mirror and seeing anything less than perfection

There being a better choice than you.

Imperfectness scares human beings

Because we want to survive.

Surviving in symmetry

But we also want to love

And love is imperfect and we like perfect things here

Love is multiple

Love is all the colors in one

Love is....

Love is everything

Love is when you look into that person's eyes

Love is a laugh with your friend

Love is crying in your bed alone

Love is deciding to get up for another day

Love is hard

Love is complicated

Love does not fit into a box

Love is energy

Constantly through the fabric of the universe and into you leaving an imprint

Why do we love?

When there will always be an end.

Because here things end.

We ourselves have a time limit

So how could love be endless?

Unbreakable?

Love is everything.

So when I say I don't know what love means to me and I don't know what love is, I think I know exactly what love is.

Love is…

Its moments and memories

Tiny breaths and wanting to stay

It's kisses and tears

Love is comfort

Love is….

Love is dangerous

Love is a high and then a sudden low

So why would I love?

Is loss the price we pay for love?

The imprints of the heart that won't disappear always
reminding you of the love you lost.

What do I say to that?

I don't know why we search for this.

I don't know why your infinite love shattered

Or maybe I do

Because even knowing all of this even knowing how
dangerous it is to love

I could never stop

Knowing

That love is…

I just keep growing

it was dark and now it's light

the seed realized

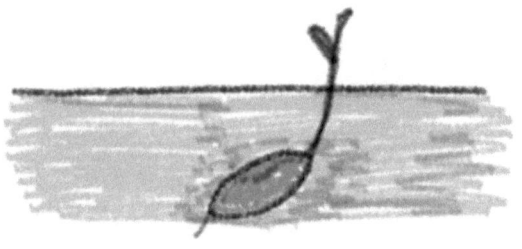

The Little Things Humans Do,

I love the little things
humans do

How we laugh when
things are funny

Or talk about our
feelings

It's adopting little
companions

Or that true squinty eyed
smile

It's how we look at
clouds and find different
shapes

Or how we can't help but
dance when a certain
sound starts to play

Its making music

And baking cookies

Kisses on foreheads

Or grabbing his hand in a
crowd

Obsessing over ice
cream

And finding shells at the
beach

The way we make
friends

Or how we build our
lives around the people
we love

It's how a hug makes
things better

Or taking photos of the
things that matter

Compliments

Holding the door

How beautiful it is the
little things humans do

Choosing a person
forever

And mini you's

Or how everyone comes
from a different place

Hiking up mountains

And going to space

It's the way we dream

And pick ourselves back
up

Caring about others

And hoping to be kind

It's the way no one looks
the same

It's falling in love

And making mistakes

It's the little things that
humans do.

I reached the peak

I'm so glad I kept going

It was all worth it

First Impressions aren't everything and normal isn't real,

First impressions aren't
everything

And normal isn't real

Crowded hallways

Passing by

Unknown destinations

Scared to walk alone

Who is the person next to
you?

Is their favorite color
green?

Do they have a cat?

Who do they love?

Are they allergic to
lemonade?

Is their favorite candy
York Peppermint
Patties?

Do they want a pet
flamingo?

How badly do they want
to travel the world?

And are they a good
listener?

Do they laugh at bad
jokes?

Did they eat today?

Have they seen Star
Wars?

Do they like receiving
letters?

Lost in the shuffle

wondering who cares

Then suddenly I bump
into you

Our eyes meet

A million unsaid words

Your crooked smile

My wrinkled nose

We were strangers once

Now I know how you take your coffee

And what music makes you dance

Your favorite color is blue

And I know how badly you want to get out of this town

A random meeting

That was exactly needed

To get to know you

The twists and turns

I'm just glad you chose me

I wasn't even looking

I would have never guessed

Unboxable people

All just trying to figure it out

It takes one meeting to change a lifetime

It was one question

One second

One look

One chance

One yes

That brought me to you

First impressions aren't everything

And normal isn't real

Standing in Love,

Authentic

Sensitive

Respectful

We communicate well

Not perfect

Falling in love

That first decision

My missing piece

Laughter

The complement

Support

Instinctive

Unconditional

No expectations

My permanent companion

The right decision

Love flows without limits

Living and growing

One thought, one heart

Unchanging

Foundations set

That unbreakable bond

Our family tree

Embracing faults

No mistakes

Honesty

Respect

Living in every moment

Perfect for each other

A continuous rush

The little things matter

Because once you fall

It just is

And suddenly you're standing instead of falling in love

Look it rose again!

It was tucked deep underneath

Both me and the sun

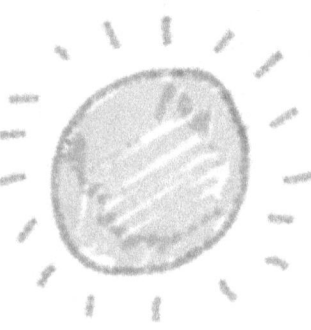

Another Multiverse,

Sometimes I wonder if in another multiverse you would find me

If things were different would we have collided?

Choices… so many choices

How could there not be another place of the different decisions?

The decision where I didn't choose to join the team

Or when she decided to stay.

That time I ran late

Or when he took a different way down the hallway after school

When we asked and you said yes or when I replied back

Do you believe in fate?

Or is there no reason?

Meant to be or just stumbled upon

It never makes any sense

Intertwined with your life

Part of my daily routine

How could you not be a part of my multiverse?

In another dimension would you recognize my smile?

The way I laugh?

The safeness of our hugs?

Would I still be scared for things to change or for you to leave?

A voice I know pulls me back and they look at me wondering where I had been

"Another world" I say but really I'm just thinking-

I'm so glad my choices led me to you.

Back in this multiverse we talked into the night and I knew in every dimension of every lifetime, we would have collided.

Golden Boy,

Flowers were blooming the day she brought him home.

He was golden. Golden like the sun.

And soft. Soft like a cloud.

There was a dozen of them, but she chose him.

On the car ride home she whispered, "I think I'll call you Hunter."

Hunter was a tornado,

destroying everything in sight,

even her favorite ballet slippers.

But she didn't care.

Embracing him with her tiny arms, she twirled him around;

He would be a dancer, too.

When it was finally time for her to go to school, he would patiently wait to play.

But as she got older the waiting got longer.

She would burst in at late hours, parents yelling

while she raced to her room without even saying hello.

But when the tears started he would hop on the bed,

curling himself in a ball, letting her stroke his golden fur so she could fall asleep.

There were many nights like this where she would cry

and wonder why the boy next door didn't notice her.

But to that dog, she was perfect, and in those moments she would start to believe him.

There came a time when she left for longer periods.

He watched as the room they once played in was put into boxes, but still he would patiently wait,

dreaming of days they would dance together on these now empty floors.

When she would come home he would burst through the door, wagging tail and all, forgetting about the time gone, just grateful she was home.

They would take long walks,

him gallivanting slower than he used to.

But when he saw his girl, it was perfect.

One time when she came home

someone came with her.

The man was taller than she was but gave good belly rubs.

He always came with her from that time on,

so now the golden boy waited for him, too.

His eyesight was becoming bad and running was tougher.

But when she came home he thought about it less

and just gave her a lick, knowing it would all be okay.

As the aching got stronger

She brought home the tiniest creature he had ever seen.

The baby was loud, but he knew this tiny bundle was important,

so he waited for the little one, too.

The little girl now danced just as he remembered.

He recognized the music.

She would laugh.

He would slowly wag his tail, lightly patting the floor where this had happened so many years ago.

The time was coming soon.

After all, dogs aren't supposed to outlive their humans.

She knew this when they brought him home that warm day,

yet still not realizing it would mean the loss of an old friend.

When he was brought to the vet they all came.

She was crying, much harder than all those years ago.

He wanted to comfort her, but moving was almost unbearable.

So with all the strength he had, he turned his head to her

and thumped his golden tail.

They were now alone, just him and her.

She played their favorite song, "Dance of the Sugar Plum Fairy," and whispered, "It's okay, you did well. Go dance in the clouds."

…

Even after Hunter passed,

whenever she was sad

she would look at the sunsets and be reminded of her golden boy.

She would hear the music and be reminded of her days with her loyal companion.

Reminded of their unconditional love.

To the Nature I've always known,

Imprints on my skin

And the voice in my head

It's in my nature to crave you

The air that demands to be held

The risk of the gambling cliffs

Transcribed in the smoke

Every passion and desire gulped into flames

It's the uneven floor and the millions of stars that call me home

To the nature I've always known.

Gave it a home,

I love you more than a dog loves a bone

I love you more than the waves love the sand

My heart is so full you gave it a home

To be loved is to be changed,

I loved the summertime but the leaves always seemed to change

falling into an auburn orange

the green wrinkling away into the familiar crunch of fall

Where I met you

youthful smile across the field.

Throwing a new plastic disk for the floppy puppy

We were young then

Kids acting like adults

Tassels barely across our faces

I once wanted to be president

But dreams change and time passes

And the jingle of bells fill the air

I meet my best friends for cocoa as I stare up at the snow coated branches

Stories of a life I have never known pour out of their mouths like we are attempting to bring each other into moments we have missed.

They are different now, I am different now

Blossoming and growing

Into the spring when the floppy puppy now a floppy dog bounded down the aisle

We had made it through the hard winter and there was finally sunshine again.

The green was back in everything

The green of us

Feeling like the kids in the field with that old broken disc

Older now, growing together

Surrounded by our entire past, faced with a future

I loved the summertime but 3 years after that spring it was different.

Floppy dog flopped his tail one last time under the giant oak in our backyard

She had gotten gray and skinny

We had loved her and now it was time to let her go

Seasons change and lives are led

Wrinkling from the years of smiles and tears

Gray from the love we shared.

Changing with the seasons

To be loved is to be changed.

To love be love is to…

To be continued...

You have reached the end but it's also the beginning. Endings have a funny way of doing that, being the moment right after a fall in which we must get up again. There has been more than one time where I didn't want to get up, I was too tired, I was ready to give up but I didn't. And I don't know for sure if it's the picking up of my pencil or little holes of light peeking in but I am so glad I did.

And if you are looking for a sign to get up, this is it. I know the darkness seems endless and the possibility of that changing seems impossible, but it can change. And there are people that care.

You will feel better. You will feel love. Because you are worth it. And if you ever need a reminder that you are,

READ THIS HERE:

You are worth it. You are worthy of another chance. You are worthy of the love you put into this world and you are worthy of every good thing you can absorb from this world.

Take it and hold on to it.

Acknowledgements

Firstly, I want to thank anyone who inspired any of the poems in The Act of Falling. Your life and your love has made me a better person, I am grateful for all of it and care for you deeply. I have learned so much from each of your stories.

Thank you to my circle of people. You make my life so full. Thank you for tirelessly reading my poems, being honest, and lifting me up when I didn't believe it was possible. Something that would be impossible is naming all these people. I promise you, there will be cookies and a handwritten letter for you.

I do however have to name my family in my gratitude—Mom, Dad, Grace, Thomas, and Anne. My rocks. There is not a day I would survive without your support. Thank you.

The other person I have to name is Amy Snapp. My mentor when I first wrote those 8 poems in my senior year and my mentor in continuing them and bringing them to you. So much Philia love for you.

And finally thank YOU. Whether this is your first time reading my words or if you have been here since I posted my first poem on Instagram or while shoved down my shyness to read them on TikTok, this book would be just an idea. I do not take the privilege of this space lightly and I celebrate you every single day.

From the bottom of my heart, thank you. I'm so glad you gave me a chance.

Index

Resources + More

You are not alone, help is available

Suicide and Crisis Helpline

- Text or call 988 for 24/7 help

Crisis Text Line

- Text TALK to 741741 to talk with a trained counselor for free 24/7 help

RAINN- National Sexual Assault Hotline

- Lifeline: 1-800-656-4673
- Chat: via hotline.rainn.org
-

National Alliance for Eating Disorders

- Helpline: 1-866-662-1235
- www.allianceforeatingdisorders.com OR www.nationaleatingdisorders.com

The Trevor Project

- Trevor Lifeline: 1-866-488-1235
- Trevor Text: text TREVOR to 1-202-304-1200

♡ The 8 Types of Love. ♡

 The people of Ancient Greece noticed long before me, that there are many different variants of love… so much so that they devised terms for them. These types of love are used to showcase how love takes on many different forms while also changing and growing. In my debut poetry project, *My Heart in Words*, I searched for these loves in my life as well as wrote 2 bookend poems before (*It's Love*) and after *(Love is…)* the project/journey.

These loves are (denoted by a drawn heart):

- Mania: obsessive love. Craving. Hurting & Loving
  - No Space for Grace
- Ludus: playful love. Flirty and crushes. Butterflies!
  - Metamorphosis
- Eros: romantic love. Physical touch & passion.
  - The Art of Hugs
- Storge: foundational love. Family & chosen family.
  - With You Wherever You Go
- Philia: friendship love. Platonic love!
  - The Years of Us
- Pragma: enduring love. Love that grows and matures over time
  - Standing in Love
- Agape: Love without asking anything in return.
  - Golden Boy
- Philautia: self-love. It is not selfish but recognizing your worth.
  - Million Little Pieces

The Research

"I'm guess I am going to have to suffer"

Sometimes I write a poem based on sole feeling and other times I write with a sure purpose and research. For this poem, I felt deeply inspired by Vincent Van Gogh's words and works. This poem is about fictional people. I wanted to create a universe and story exploring feelings that weren't completely mine. Below are the quotes and paintings that are built into the elements of the poem.

The works:

- Starry night
- Sunflowers
- Irises
- Daisies and poppies
- A pair of shoes
- A meadow in the mountains

Vincent Van Gogh Quotes:

- "The more you love, the more you suffer"
- "It is good to love many things, for therein lies strength, and whosoever loves much performs much, and can accomplish much, and what is done with love is well done"
- "I don't know anything with certainty, but seeing the stars makes me dream. "

- "There is nothing more truly artistic than to love people"
- "The fishermen know that the sea is dangerous and the storm terrible, but they have never found these dangers sufficient reason for remaining ashore. "
- One may have a blazing hearth in one's soul and yet no one ever came to sit by it. Passers-by see only a wisp of smoke from the chimney and continue on their way."
- "What would life be if we had no courage to attempt anything? "
- "I often think that the night is more alive and more richly colored than the day. "
- "Find things beautiful as much as you can, most people find too little beautiful" .
- "I missed you the first few days, and it was strange for me not to find you when I came home in the afternoon.
- "Great things are not done by impulse, but by a series of small things brought together. "
- "Love is the best and most noble thing in the human heart, especially when it has been tried and tested in life like gold in the fire"

About the author.

@piecesbyizz | piecesbyiz@gmail.com | https://isabellanewman25.wixsite.com/my-site-1

Isabella (often known as Izzy) Newman is a twenty-something year old poet who started sharing her poetry online in 2021. "The Act of Falling" is her first book which she self-published and marketed by herself and with the undying support of the ones who love her! Some things that are poetry to Izzy are ice cream in the summer, a drive with the windows down, and the human experience. Izzy just hopes that by sharing her poetry she can make at least one person feel less alone, feel a little bit of love, and be inspired to give it too. She is eternally grateful you chose to pick up this book and hold her heart delicately with such grace.

I'm proud of the life I am living.

I'm proud of the people in my life.

I'm proud of me for trying.

I'm proud of me for loving even when it's hard.

I'm proud of me for healing.

I'm proud of me for growing.

I'm proud that I keep going.

I'm proud of me.

2:14 am